Oil Lamps A G
And C...

Myles Bevis

The following guide is intended to be used purely for information and educational purposes. Oil lamps can be dangerous which is pointedly mentioned in this book. It is purely and absolutely the reader's, or individual's personal decision to light an oil lamp and the author will accept no responsibility for any damage or injury caused in any way from the operation of oil lamps. For safeties sake never leave a lit oil lamp unattended and always extinguish before leaving any area where one may be operating. It is prudent for me to advise you to only use oil lamps for decorative purposes and never fill them with oil and light them.

Contents

Introduction

READERS BEWARE!

Let me offer a serious word of warning before you delve into the innards of this guide.

OIL LAMPS ARE HIGHLY ADDICTIVE!

'Rubbish!' I hear you declare. How can an archaic method of producing not particularly bright light be addictive?'

Well, take my word for it. They are! Completely, absolutely and totally habit forming.

Once you have purchased your first shabby old brass table oil lamp, polished off 100 years of grime so it sparkles and reflects your room in strange distorted images. Once you have cleaned the dirty clogged up burner and air vents and replaced the wick. Once you have lit it and seen a one hundred and twenty year old object functioning and producing light as once it did when brand new and proud.... It is too late! You've returned an item of functional beauty back to life. The feeling of satisfaction is substantial!

You'll buy another... and then another...!

Will that be enough?

Absolutely no chance whatsoever. It's too late, my friend! YOU'RE HOOKED!

Next step for you... Oil Lamps Anonymous!

So, this major point being cleared up, on with the business.

Let There Be Light!

Over the many years I have been operating my Oil Lamp website, the most frequently asked question from my customers has been. 'How do I use my oil lamp?'

And what an important question this is! After all oil lamps are fuelled by oil. Oil is inflammable and therefore incredibly dangerous if not used correctly. The plain fact is, people have actually lost lives through the incorrect use of their oil lamps over the centuries!

So to answer this most important of questions, years ago I quickly knocked out some brief notes on safety and operation which I still send to every person who purchases an oil lamp from me now.

Operating and caring for an oil lamp is not like the simple act of turning on a switch and having instant light. There are necessary rituals to perform and lighting and preparing to light an oil lamp is anything but instant. Because of this I promised myself, however, one day I would write a book containing more comprehensive information on this most important subject and also include a brief history of lighting by oil and descriptions of the different types of domestic lamp in use today.

This 'One Day' has finally arrived and the result is 'Oil Lamps A Guide To Their Care And Operation.' I hope you will find the book interesting as well as useful and informative.

Oil Lamps A Very Brief History

You may wonder how long artificial lighting has been around. The answer is, probably a lot longer than you thought.

The first kind of artificial lighting came with the discovery of fire. Fire produced light and warmth throughout the long hours of the dark and dangerous night. You may be surprised to hear this world changing discovery is thought to originate during the times of Homo Erectus in the region of 400,000 years ago!

Fire was the only means of night time illumination for many thousands of years from then onwards and would have led towards socialising and eventually the origins of night time 'stories round the fire'. Light from portable fire in the shape of flaming torches would have been used extensively during these prehistoric millennia.

How long have oil lamps been around for?

Would you believe, over 70,000 years?

Incredible, isn't it!

Palaeolithic cave dwellers observed animal fat burned, probably by watching drips from spit roasted animals spitting and flaring as they fell into the fire below.

Hollowed out stones - oil lamps in their simplest form - have been dated back all that time and found to have been receptacles for moss drenched with oil or animal fat and lit. Rather smelly and smoky, you may well surmise, but nevertheless a viable method of producing light. This is the lighting method talented Stone Age artists would have illuminated walls with to produce the remarkable cave pictures in Lascaux in France's picturesque Dordogne area and others all over the world.

Over the centuries since those dim and dingy years many receptacles have been used for holding oil to make light. Sea shell lamps dating back to 4,000 BC have been found in the ruins of Ur in Mesopotamia, now Iraq. These would have been used in a similar way to the early stone lamps or with oil and a floating piece of bark or similar for a wick. A variety of different shells such as oyster or scallop were used all over the Mediterranean areas and islands. These would have held vegetable or castor oil with a material wick, or the very useful burning bark chips floating on top.

As well as stone and shell ancient oil lamps have been made from many different materials including pottery, bronze, brass, iron, porcelain, coconuts, sea urchins, chalk and many other more obscure methods.

Oily fish and birds have actually been used to produce light. Storm petrels – dead I hasten to add - with string wicks threaded through the body were burnt in the Orkney Islands until the beginning of the 20th century, and Candle fish held in split sticks with slivers of bark for wick were used in Alaska!

Popular from Roman times Spout Lamps survived until well into the nineteenth century. These could be made from brass, or more cheaply from tin. Little Roman pottery spout lamps still abound as many millions were made. They frequently appear featured on online auctions and cost no more than the price of a meal out for two. Many metal spout lamps fitted on a stand and consisted of an oil reservoir with one or two upward facing spouts at the top. Wicks were inserted in the spouts reaching into the reservoirs to absorb the fuel oil and lit to provide light. In coastal regions the main fuel would have been whale oil. Colza - rape seed - oil was also used and olive oil in Mediterranean areas. The 'Aladdin' lamp of 'Arabian Nights' fame was a single wick spout lamp.

The Lampe Lucerna sometimes termed 'Venetian Reading Lamp,' was also a spout lamp having upwards of three spouts. The spout part of the lamp was fixed centrally to a stand where it could slide up and down. Lucerna were popular in Europe, especially Italy and southern Europe and were in use from the seventeen hundreds to later in the nineteenth century.

The first exciting major change to lighting technology which had remained more or less static for thousands of years came towards the end of the eighteenth century. In 1780 the Swiss Aimé Argand used scientific principles to invent what was to be the forerunner of the central draft oil lamp.

Argand took a flat wick and fitted it between two metal tubes one inside the other to form a round shape. The lamp was designed so air could pass through the center of the inner tube which when passing over the inside of the raised wick produced a flame of considerably more brilliance than a more conventional lamp. When later a glass bottle with no base was placed over the burner it caused air to be drawn through the tube much faster and the brilliance of the flame to increase dramatically along with a considerable reduction in smoke emission.

Although this was a far reaching invention, a milestone in fact, there was a drawback. The only satisfactory fuel available at the time for these lamps was whale oil, or the sticky Colza oil or in fact any vegetable oil, which didn't soak up the wick from below with any satisfaction. To remedy this problem, higher than wick oil reservoirs were introduced to drip feed through a tube to the bottom of the burner. The result was a lamp that produced a brighter flame than had ever been seen before, but which was top heavy and used a substantial amount of fuel.

Moderator lamps were introduced based on Argand's burner. These had an oil reservoir below the burner and fuel was pumped upwards by a clockwork motor releasing a compressed spring to operate a leather covered piston. The Moderator was patented in 1835 and was still in popular use at the end of the century.

Then came the great change. The change which was to completely revolutionise the quality of artificial light.

In 1847 a Scotsman, James Young discovered how to refine paraffin. Paraffin had been discovered in 1830 but was of no major significance until the refining process was introduced. In 1850 James Young patented his process and things were really on the way at last. The era of the paraffin (kerosene) lamp as still used today had begun.

The great names of oil lamp manufacture such as Hinks, Messenger's, Evered, Young's, Palmer, Veritas and many more were based in the UK, many in the great industrial midland metropolis of Birmingham.

In 1865 Joseph Hinks placed two flat wicks side by side and invented the duplex, or twin wick, oil lamp burner. Since then oil lighting has never been the same and some of the most sought after oil lamps now in the world were manufactured at his UK factory close to the center of Birmingham. Every genuine collector of flat wick oil lamps strives to have at least one oil lamp by this prestigious manufacturer in their collections. People in the UK seemed to favour flat wick lamps over the more complex center draft variety which was much more popular in Europe.

Both type of lamp were, as well as being household lighting essentials, a pleasure to look at. Mass produced as well as top of the range oil lamps could be elegant and beautiful. We recognise this now, and these once discarded incredible items of lighting history have, at last, become highly collectable and sought after.

Both types of lamp were also popular in the USA although the central draft burners were more highly favored and makers such as Edward Miller of Connecticut and Plume & Atwood again of Connecticut excelled.

The Main Types Of Oil Lamp

Oil lamps come in many different shapes and sizes, but on the whole conform to just a few basic types. In this guide I am concentrating on domestic lighting but there are other types i.e. mining lamps, railway lamps, vehicle lamps etc.

Below are listed the principal versions of domestic oil lamp and a description of how they operate.

- Flat wick side draft oil lamps

- Tubular wick center draft oil lamps

- Lamps with flat wicks forced into round tubes

- Non pressure lamps with mantles

- Pressure lamps with mantles

Flat wick side draft oil lamps

Flat wick side draft oil lamps came in a huge variety of sizes and shapes and taking much varied wick widths from ¼ inch to 1½ inches.

Very much favored in the UK the illustration to the right is of an antique duplex burner with two side by side flat wicks each having a width of 1-1/16 inches.

Illustrated in its open position this particular burner is a top of the range model which has an important feature. The top section can be raised by sliding a key lever thus enabling easy lighting without the need to remove the chimney and shade. Standard duplex burners, as in the next photo, did not have this feature although most had a sliding mechanism to raise over the wicks in order to snuff out the flames.

The draft enters through the air intake holes round the circumference of the burner and then through an inner mesh bug filter before passing over the wicks and up through the chimney. The illumination provided is a nice soft light but not exceptionally bright.

Tubular wick center draft oil lamps

Center draft lamps also came in a variety of wick sizes from 13/16 of an inch in diameter to 2¾ inches diameter. The burners which were fitted with tubular wicks slotted over an air intake tube which ran right through the center of the lamp and air intake holes were located either in the base or a waisted part of the stand as in the photo to the right. In order for them to function correctly they had to be used in conjunction with a flame spreader which slotted into the top of the central air tube.

Center draft lamps because of their design could produce up to 200 candlepower of light output, which was massive for the time, almost the same brightness as a proper 60 watt electric bulb - not to be confused with the new politically correct low wattage things!

An interesting further development of this type of oil lamp was the addition of an incandescent mantle as used by the Aladdin Lamp Company, Edward Miller & Company and a few others.

Lamps with flat wicks forced into round tubes

Invented by Wild & Wessel of Berlin in 1865 the Kosmos burner was a hybrid between flat wick and central draft lamp. A wide flat wick was wound into a tube to emerge at the top as a round shape. Operating from a side draft which also directed air up the center of the wick tube meant a flame spreader wasn't necessary and there were also fewer parts to put together. The burner top was narrower than the base to help the air flow and the instantly recognisable Kosmos chimney was stepped in just above the flame to assure the correct air flow.

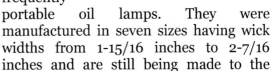

These burners gave a bright high quality flame and were mainly used for smaller and frequently portable oil lamps. They were manufactured in seven sizes having wick widths from 1-15/16 inches to 2-7/16 inches and are still being made to the present day – although not in all the original wick widths.

Working on the same principles as Kosmos burners and looking much alike the Matador burner had a parallel width wick tube and also a flame spreader. The Matador chimney, however was different to the Kosmos in that instead of being stepped it had a short round bulge close to the base.

Development continued over the years and in 1884 a Kosmos burner with a flame spreader was patented. In the UK this was

marketed as the 'Globe Vulcan' and in the USA the 'Imperial.' These average sized lamps were exceptional and could produce as much light as the expensive to run high output European center draft burners. The chimney was most unusual in that it had the Kosmos step above the burner and then above that another bulge where the top of

the flame spreader reposed. The bottom section served as a flame box which was usually concealed within the interior of more conventional burners.

Center draft lamps with mantles

A new development in oil lamp technology came when it was found in

1885 the placing of a specially coated mantle over a center draft burner set up to produce a blue flame caused the mantle to glow brightly,

substantially increasing the light output of a lamp. Non pressure mantle lamps were manufactured by Aladdin, Edward Miller, Juno and a number of other companies. At the time of writing Aladdin lamps can still be purchased new and produce a nice white light 10 times more powerful than a duplex twin wick burner. A properly maintained non pressure mantle lamp will burn brightly without odor or noise.

Pressure Lamps With Mantles

Pressure lamps are more complex in operation than the wick variety. They operate by pressurising the fuel reservoir with a hand pump, thus driving the paraffin into a gas generator. The vapor burns and heats an incandescent mantle until it glows. The quality of light produced is high and bright. There are certain disadvantages such as the need to pump more pressure in now and then, and the lamps also burn with a hissing noise.

Famous names are Tilley, Vapalux and Bialladin, although there were many more on the market. The model illustrated is an early Tilley.

A Site For Your Oil Lamp

You'll find oil lamps are relatively simple to look after, but for those who may never have actually put match to wick in this age of instant lighting, for safeties sake there are a few precautions you need to know about and be sure of before actually lighting up your lamp.

Paraffin (Kerosene in the USA) lamps work on the principle of vapor, produced by fuel absorbed into the fabric of a wick by capillary action, burning in oxygen. The thing to note is it's really the vapor which should burn rather than the actual wick, although, as perfection is yet to be achieved, wicks are bound to char and gradually burn down over time. If the wick is actually physically glowing and burning it means the flame has been turned up to such an extent it could become a dangerous fire hazard.

Traditionally wick has been woven from cotton, but arguably nowadays an equally good flame can be produced from correctly used wicks woven from fibreglass! Fibreglass, to the best of my knowledge, is not flammable so goes to prove the point it is actually fuel vapor which is burning rather than the wick fabric when an oil lamp is used as it is meant to be.

Finding a site for your oil lamp

A nicely maintained functioning oil lamp is an object of practical beauty which will give you much pleasure over the years. There are a few points to remember though.

As well as light another by product of a working oil lamp is heat. Oil lamps produce heat. The chimney is not just a way of drawing air over a flame; it is also the method by which considerable heat is dissipated. So you should give more than a little thought as to where you will site your oil lamp.

Places which could present a fire hazard, such as near curtains or where anything can be blown over the chimney – net curtains, blinds etc - you should obviously avoid and also anywhere where children or pets have access to. Over the years I have supplied hundreds of chimneys and many replacement glass shades to unfortunate people whose rampaging cats have skittled their oil lamps. I am, of course, most grateful to these benevolent animals, but seriously... if the lamps had been lit at the time and fuel oil liberally flowing everywhere...??

Think also about how high your oil lamp will be. If it is less than 1 metre below the ceiling the hot exhaust from the chimney could be a fire hazard, especially if you are burning a mantle lamp. If your lamp is of the hanging variety which will most likely place it closer to the ceiling make sure you have a smoke bell placed directly a few inches above the chimney to dissipate the heat.

An oil lamp makes a great dining table centerpiece. Sideboards or low display cabinet tops are ideal. What could be better than an ornate Victorian lamp in the center of the mantelpiece? Or maybe a pair – one at each end?

How does one carry an oil lamp? Very simply, one hand holding the stand, the other supporting the base. It is tempting to cup both hands round the fuel reservoir and lift but a dangling heavy stand and base could eventually cause plaster of paris fount connections to loosen and cause damage or breakage to the lamp. I think it's safe to say nobody wants their furnishings or carpets saturated by lamp oil.

Operating Your Oil Lamp

The first step towards operating your oil lamp is to acquire the correct type of fuel. The fuel which Victorian oil lamps were designed to burn is simply ordinary Paraffin or as titled in the USA Kerosene. Although lamps function very well with this fuel paraffin does tend to burn with an odor. There are now a variety of more refined versions of paraffin on the market which burn with less or no odor so if you would prefer a more home friendly fuel you could try a few different makes to see which suits your lamps best. As a rule paraffin gives the best flame quality but I'm assured some of the more refined versions are excellent.

Paraffin is a clear liquid and available from most good hardware or specialist shops. There are a number of websites who offer the more refined lamp oil. Just call on Google.

Two Important Warnings

- ***NEVER* USE OR TRY TO USE PETROL (GASOLINE) AS OIL LAMP FUEL! *EXPLOSIVE DISASTER IS ASSURED!***

- ***NEVER* TOUCH THE CHIMNEY OF A LIT OR RECENTLY DOUSED OIL LAMP. SERIOUS BURNS COULD RESULT!**

Filling your oil lamp

You may consider the straightforward act of pouring paraffin into a lamp fount is the simplest thing in the world. Surely you just remove the burner or cap and pour the liquid in, reseal the thing and light it?

Afraid not!

There is one very necessary precaution to take.

NEVER fill your lamp to the top!

Why?

Because you'd be causing a serious fire hazard!

As an oil lamp reaches its operating temperature and the paraffin in the fount warms up the liquid expands. If it is filled right to the top this expansion will force fuel out of anywhere it can emerge from, usually from the burner area and if the worst comes to the worst a fire could result.

To be safe never fill the lamp over ¾ of its capacity and make sure the filling aperture is screwed or fitted correctly before lighting the lamp.

If your lamp is dry or being fuelled for the first time leave it for at least 20 minutes to enable the wick to fully absorb the paraffin.

Use the following procedure to light your lamp and it should present no problems and give you long and faithful service.

- Remove the chimney.

- Adjust the wick so that 1mm is showing above its holder (the holder is the burner part the wick actually emerges from, not any covers or a duplex split burner top)

- Light the wick.

- Replace the chimney, and shade if there is one.

- Leave the lamp for **AT LEAST** 10 minutes, preferably 20 minutes if you have enough patience, until it has approached its operating temperature.

- Gradually over a period of at least another 10 minutes adjust the wick to its optimum running height – the height at which it gives the best required illumination without smoking – usually when about 3mm is showing above the wick holder.

Please note, for some Kosmos burners the optimum height above the wick tube can be as little as 1mm.

To extinguish an oil lamp is also quite a ritual. Turn the flame down to its starting height so the light is very low. Then place your hand, angled slightly downwards behind the top of the chimney. Blow right across the chimney top at your hand. A good sharp puff will douse the flame.

Don't turn the flame down until it goes out in case the wick travels too far down the tube and disengages from the adjustment mechanism.

Most duplex twin flat wick burners have a device which by depressing a lever will cause a mechanism to rise and close over the wicks thereby snuffing them out. If you like to use this method remember to first turn the flame down to its lowest before using the snuffer. Personally I prefer not to use the mechanical method and just blow over the chimney into a hand. A number of central draft burners also have snuffers. Some are extremely complex and operate a diaphragm very similar to a camera stopping down system.

A properly adjusted flame should never smoke and the wick should not char more than a little at the tip. Remember if your lamp smokes it is burning too high. Most oil lamps will never be able to give out as much light as an electric bulb so it is unfair to ask too much of them.

Wicks and Mantles

Never adjust a wick when it is dry. Turning the adjustment screw on a dry wick, especially one which has not been used for a while, could cause it to tear and become unusable. The lamp fuel acts as a lubricant enabling wicks to be freely adjusted.

Having a charred and uneven wick that smokes is a sign your lamp has probably been used with too high a flame which has caused the actual wick fabric to burn more than it should normally. Another cause of this problem could be a blocked air vent or bug filter. Check these at regular intervals to make sure air flows freely.

A charred wick will need trimming. For flat wick burners, when the lamp is cold turn up the wick and using **sharp** scissors cut straight across and just below the charred area making sure the cut is even and there are no stray threads.

The best way to trim a circular wick is to use a circular trimming device. These are not always easily available though so another method is to turn up the wick until it can be pinched flat at the top. Then cut straight across the double thickness in a similar way to the flat wick method. Turn the wick down and if any slightly higher areas become visible, carefully snip them until all is even.

If your oil lamp is of the variety which uses a heated mantle to produce incandescence, great care is needed as just a touch to a burnt in mantle can cause it to disintegrate. Even when installing a new mantle only touch the wire or metal frame and never the fabric.

A mantle is a cone shaped fabric mesh impregnated with rare earth oxides which have the capacity to glow when heated.

To replace a mantle first remove the old one by turning the holder anticlockwise to unlock it and then withdrawing the unit. To install a new one simply reverse this procedure, making sure it is correctly locked in place.

Without touching the mesh apply a lit match to the bottom of the cone. This will fire the mantle by burning off the fabric and leaving an extremely brittle rare earth framework ready for use.

Chimneys

Oil lamp chimneys are made from glass. A rather obvious comment you may think, but you need to realise glass is an extremely fickle material. A particular quality of glass is that when heated it expands. The faster it is heated, the quicker it expands. Conversely, when cooled it contracts in just the same way. Because of this quality if you want to retain your chimney for many years, or until smashed by a household accident it needs to be treated with care and respect.

If your chimney is heated up too quickly the expansion which occurs will not be even. Different areas will expand quicker than others. Glass being a brittle substance the result of this conflict of expansion rates **WILL** cause a crack or two to appear. In extreme circumstances a too rapidly heated chimney can shatter or actually explosively disintegrate!

Antique chimneys, if the lamp is gently brought up to operating temperature as previously described, should function well, but if not are prone to instant decomposition, especially if the lamp is being operated at a higher than optimum light output.

Modern chimneys have much more heat resistant qualities but still require to be gently brought up to operating temperature. They still need to be treated with respect. Do this and they will give you good service.

The world was bigger and everything slower in the days when oil lamps were new. To realise this, slowing down and taking things easy will make all the difference.

When fitting or replacing a lamp's chimney it should fit easily and smoothly behind the chimney clasps. In Victorian times nothing was a completely standard size and sometimes the thickness of glass varied making some chimney bases slightly wider than others. Because of this, chimney clasps were designed to be bendable when slight inward or outward pressure was applied.

If the chimney you are fitting is a little too tight a fit just gently ease the holder clasps very slightly outwards until the chimney will slot in and out easily making sure it is still a good firm fit. If too loose, just adjust the holders a little the opposite direction.

Some twin flat wick burners you will find have been fitted with a chimney which has a slightly flatter bulge than others. You can also use a round bulge chimney just as effectively. If your lamp's chimney has an oval bulge make sure you position it so the oval length runs parallel to the width of the wicks. If fitted incorrectly the chimney could blacken or crack if the flames are too high. The oval chimneys are becoming harder to find these days but are still available. It is said that the flatter bulge encourages a slightly faster air passage over the twin wicks which in turn could provide a brighter flame. Personally, although it is nice to have a choice, I have never been able to note a significant difference in light quality!

Burner Maintenance

Over time, especially with flat wick lamps, you could notice your wick flames may be beginning to lose quality, produce a reduced light and smoke when at normal operating height. Usually this problem can be remedied by trimming the wick, but if it still persists try the following. Check the metal gauze air filter inside your burner is not clogged with dust and debris. As a rule most flat wick burners can be accessed by gently easing the top section and removing it. Some very basic duplex burners can appear to be a one piece unit. You will find, however, it is possible to prise the wick cover up from inside the chimney clasps. If you don't want to do this, washing the burner could also clean the internal filter. Remove the wicks and shake the burner vigorously in hot water with a generous amount of dishwashing liquid added. Rinse well with fast flowing water, shake thoroughly outside, then give it a good blow through with a hair dryer until it is completely dry inside. Replace the wicks and all being well it should function correctly again.

If the problem persists try a different lamp oil. Finding the best make to suit a particular lamp can make all the difference.

An Extra Note On 'Vulkan' Burners

Since publishing this book, I've received a few questions about how to operate these unique burners without causing the hard to find, expensive, special chimneys to crack and shatter, so here are a few notes on how to go about this safely.

The Vulkan Kosmos was a cleverly invented state of the art burner designed to give a higher light output than more conventional oil lamps of the day. However, because of the uniqueness of this burner it does need a little more care and attention when lighting it up than the average 'bog standard' oil lamp.

Most conventional oil lamps have the 'flame box' inside the brass part of the burner where the wick emerges from the wick tube or sheath. The Vulkan has an extra long flame spreader because it actually has the flame box incorporated in the extra base section of the glass chimney and so it is advisable to warm the chimney very gently before turning the wick up to its operating height.

Following are a few essential hints on lighting and warming procedure.

- Never use the burner without the flame spreader in position.

- Light the wick at the lowest height at which it will burn.

- When lit replace the chimney and leave the wick at the starting height for at least 10 minutes for the chimney to warm.

- After 10 minutes – or more if wished – turn the wick up very slightly and leave for a further 10 minutes to assure all the glass has expanded evenly.

- After this second 10 minutes gently turn the wick up to its operating height. If there is any smoke produced the wick is too high and could crack the chimney so turn down quickly.

- Make sure the wick is always adjusted or trimmed so it is an even height at all times.

If these steps are adhered to the existing chimney should last a long time.

Vulkan chimneys can sometimes be found on eBay. The flat wick is 90mm wide and can also be found sometimes on eBay or by 'Googling'.

There is a specialist company 'Miles Stair's Wick Shop' who commission these special chimneys made from Borosilicate and they also supply wick. At the time of publishing the following URL will send you to their correct page http://www.milesstair.com/CHIMNEYS.html and the type of chimney needed is the 'Imperial / Globe Vulkan Chimney' with 2-7/16" base fitting.

Aladdin Mantle Lamps

Over the years I've received a great many questions on how to use Aladdin Mantle Lamps so here is a whole chapter dedicated to the operation of these exceptional producers of mellow high quality light.

The Aladdin oil lamp is especially favored in areas or places where there is no electricity or where power is only supplied at certain times of the day and a good functional light is required. They are generally not purchased by avid collectors of Victorian lamps where the spectacular beauty is of more value than the actual light output, and so their second hand value is remarkably low for such marvellous producers of bright light. Aladdin mantle lamps can also still be purchased new and unused.

A correctly operating Aladdin mantle lamp will operate without odor or noise and produces a full 60 candle power – equal to the light produced by 10 standard duplex (twin flat wick) oil lamps.

The first point to mention is Aladdin oil lamps do not function quite like conventional oil lamp burners where the brightness is derived directly from the wick.

The Aladdin burner is designed to mix fuel vapor with air in the ratio of 1 to 16. This produces a blue flame which then heats up a mantle impregnated with rare earth elements to produce a satisfying bright but mellow glow. It is a light quite good enough to satisfactorily read a book by without straining your eyes.

An Aladdin wick correctly used will produce hundreds of hours of light and a reservoir of lamp oil will give at least 10 hours of continuous illumination.

Things to know before lighting your Aladdin lamp

- As with flat wick oil lamps **never** overfill the oil reservoir. Make sure the lamp oil is never higher than ½ inch below the filler cap, lower in summer as the oil will expand with heat.

- Always operate the lamp with the pepper pot flame spreader installed in the top of the air supply tube.

- When your wick needs trimming it is essential you **always** use the special Aladdin circular trimming tool. If you don't have one they are readily available on a variety of Aladdin spares websites. To use the trimmer first take off the gallery and turn the wick down until it's level with the top of the outer tube. Remove the flame spreader and fit the trimmer in its place. Gently turn up the wick until it just engages with the trimmer then gently and carefully twist it *clockwise* until the wick carbon is nice and even and all the same height with no straggly bits. Carefully clean any carbon debris before replacing the gallery. **Never** try and trim with scissors.

- Check the fuel level at regular intervals and *always fill with oil at room temperature.* Filling with cold oil from an outside store room and lighting the lamp can immediately cause spitting and damage the mantle.

Charring The Wick

An absolute essential with an Aladdin lamp when a new wick has been fitted is to make sure you pre char it correctly. A wick needs to be charred correctly before first use in order to produce a good even blue flame. If this is not done, or done incorrectly, you will never have a perfectly operating lamp.

Follow these steps and your lamp should function perfectly.

- Install new wick making sure you *leave it totally dry*.

- Remove the gallery and un-slot and remove the flame spreader.

- Turn the wick up and let it project about 4mm above the outer wick tube.

- Pour a small quantity of lamp oil into a jar top or similar, then dip the projecting 4mm of wick into this for about 5 seconds.

- Let the wick drip free of excess lamp oil then turn the burner upright again and light the wick. Let the wick burn itself out completely – usually after about 4 or 5 minutes.

- When the wick is totally out and cold again with absolutely no sign of any smouldering gently use the wick trimmer as described before.

- Replace the flame spreader and gallery. You are now ready at last to light your lamp.

Lighting Your Aladdin

If this is the first time you are going to light your Aladdin it is now time to fill with lamp oil. Remove the filler cap and gently pour in the oil until it is *no higher than ½ an inch below the aperture.*

Leave the lamp for at least one hour for the wick to fully absorb the lamp oil. This is only necessary when the lamp has been filled for the first time or has been stored empty for some time.

Now without touching the fabric carefully fit the mantle by holding the frame and twisting gently clockwise to insert into the slots on the gallery.

If you have installed a new mantle apply a match flame to the mantle's base – without touching the mantle fabric with the match. This will burn off the fabric and leave the rare earth lattice ready to perform. Then fit the chimney.

Follow the steps below to light your lamp.

- Gently remove the gallery complete with mantle and chimney.

- Raise the wick until it is about 4mm above the outer wick tube.

- Light the wick and wait until the flame has spread all round. Carefully replace the gallery unit and gently lock into place.

- Remember, nothing can be instant with oil lamps and gradually turn the wick up until the mantle is *partially* glowing. Then leave the lamp to warm up for between 10 and 15 minutes.

- Slowly turn the wick up until about three quarters of the mantle is glowing *then leave it*, as heat builds up the mantle will become fully illuminated with no further physical aid.

- To douse the lamp first turn the wick right down until the mantle is no longer glowing. Place a hand behind the chimney top and blow across the chimney. *Do not blow directly down the chimney* as this could shatter the delicate mantle.

When the lamp is operating if flame can be seen passing through the mantle the wick is too high and should be turned down until all flame is within the mantle.

If the mantle blackens or black spots appear this also means the flame is too high. Turn it down right away and the marks will gradually burn off. Please observe these rules as, believe me, the last thing you want is to have to deal with a runaway uncontrollable oil lamp!

An Aladdin lamp should never be left alone in a room burning at its full capacity. Turn the lamp down until all incandescence has left the mantle first, or even better, extinguish it completely.

If you do extinguish the lamp when leaving a room, make sure to let the chimney and gallery cool down before re-lighting. Serious burns can occur when touching hot lamp parts!

Glass Shades

There are many different sizes and shapes of glass oil lamp shades. Most, however, were based on variations of the types illustrated below.

Above is a glass cranberry antique open tulip shade and to the right a typical antique clear etched glass globe shade.

Left is a glass cranberry closed tulip shade and below an antique etched clear glass closed tulip - nowadays sometimes inaccurately described as a 'beehive.'

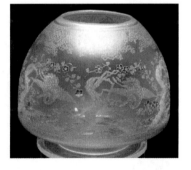

Contrary to many people's opinions there was no hard and fast rule as to what type of shade should go with a particular lamp. In the distant days when oil lamps were new and an essential part of every household the choice of shade type – if indeed a shade was required at all - was personal to the taste of the purchaser. A wide selection of shades were offered as extras although lamps would have been featured in shop displays complete with particular shades in place. Many people would have chosen the type illustrated.

Below are a variety illustrating the beauty of glass Victorian and Edwardian oil lamp shades.

 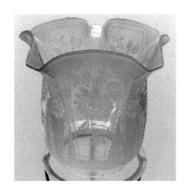

Care And Cleaning

Some oil lamp collectors will never actually fill their lamps with oil and use them for lighting purposes. The intrinsic decorative quality is all their requirement is.

Other collectors will avidly use their lamps at every opportunity possible and take enormous pleasure in being able to use and operate a Victorian oil lamp just as was intended by the manufacturers over 100 years ago.

Whichever category you fit into, your lamps will every now and then need cleaning.

In the so called 'good old days' every home of note would have had a lamp man. A man whose sole duty would be to clean, fill, wick trim, polish and repair all of the large amount of oil lamps an up market residence would have. You could estimate at least five oil lamps to a room! Imagine how many oil lamps could be in an entrance hall, 3 or 4 reception rooms, dining room, library, drawing rooms, billiards room, stairways, kitchen, upwards of 5 bedrooms and servants quarters! As John Wayne would have said... 'That's one hell of a lot of oil lamps mister!'

Even ordinary middle class homes before WW1 would have had at least one servant whose duties would have included the dreaded oil lamp!

These days, I'm afraid, we have to do it ourselves!

Brasswork will tarnish eventually. Chimneys will become dusty and if used regularly will over time acquire a transparent oily film inside, or if they are being used incorrectly blacken with soot.

Remember glass is a fickle material so take care when washing it. The following are the rules I personally stick to when washing glass chimneys and expensive antique shades, and have achieved good results.

- Never wash chimneys, shades or any other glass oil lamp parts in a dishwasher.

- Never wash chimneys, shades or any other glass oil lamp parts in hot water.

- Never try to wash a hot chimney straight from a recently extinguished oil lamp. Invariably it will shatter on entering the water. Let it first cool to room temperature.

- Use a plastic washing up bowl with *cool* water and a normal amount of dishwashing detergent.

- Use a conventional washing up brush with care for the outside of chimneys and also inside and outside shades. Use a bottlebrush to clean inside chimneys. If chimneys are sooted up a little cream cleaner on the bottlebrush should solve the problem.

- Rinse in clean cool water and dry with paper towels or washing up cloth. I always wear rubber or latex gloves for these operations to avoid finger printing lovely clean sparkling glass.

Brass parts, stands, bases etc can either be left to acquire a patina or they can be polished to a bright finish. There is no standard. This is entirely up to the owner.

Many different makes of metal polish, some extremely expensive, are on the market. Personally I find for most brass cleaning purposes 'Brasso' wadding is ideal.

If your lamp has brass parts with a patina or you are letting a recently restored item acquire one, a quick wipe over and a light buffing with spray on furniture polish will give a lovely lustrous look. Glass founts also are perfect subjects for this treatment.

If you want the brass parts of a newly restored lamp to stay bright and really don't want to have the bother of polishing you can use the following procedure on all except burners.

Wearing rubber or latex gloves to ensure no fingerprints or grease will reach the brass, using a paper towel thoroughly clean and degrease the area with methylated spirit then thoroughly dry with another paper towel. Using masking tape mask off any areas not to be affected. Then using a clear acrylic lacquer *spray sparingly* over the cleaned brasswork. Leave for half an hour and repeat.

This should last for years keeping your brass nice and bright, especially if now and then you buff over it with a dry cloth which has been used with spray on furniture polish.

Old or new lacquer can be removed with ordinary paint stripper. Please wear protective clothing and rubber gloves.

Burners also should be kept clean as previously mentioned. Every now and then, or when trimming wicks you could wipe the metal over with a methylated spirit impregnated rag to degrease and then buff over with a dry cloth.

Restoration

Many serious lamp collectors purchase a fully restored, completely cleaned pristine and perfectly working oil lamp. As close as it could possibly be to when it was originally offered to the public in a variety of venues, from ordinary hardware shops to the great names in prestigious capital city department stores. This is the type of lamp I have been proud to offer my customers over the years.

Every oil lamp featured in this book, in fact, is one which I have personally sourced and fully restored myself over the space of quite a few years. All are now being cared for by people in a variety of countries who I know will treat them with love and respect.

Dedicated collectors purchase, as I do, sorry looking pieces of black oily smelly things in a variety of broken pieces which were once wonderful working objects of functional beauty. These dirty, sticky, blackened quite revolting old pieces of rubbish are lovingly dissembled, degreased, cleaned, repaired with parts from other beyond repair lamps or specially made parts, silver soldered, and amazingly after many, many, hours of toil and attention brought back to life as items of wonderful functional beauty.

For many of these dedicated people, fuel oil will never again be introduced into the founts of the carefully restored masterpieces. They will be polished and dusted and given pride of place in prominent places and be forever admired for the wonderful objects they are.

I'm all in favour of that. My few personal remaining rescued works of beautiful lighting history deserve to be kept clean, perfect and pristine. The few lamps I keep in hand for power cuts are well maintained brass servant's quarter lamps. They are just blackened brass lamps with well maintained burners and wicks with clean fuel which produce just as high quality light as something worth eight or nine hundred pounds more than they do!

Many other collectors will delight in using their newly restored antique pieces for the purpose they were designed for as often and frequently as possible.

Whichever category you fall into, if you decide to purchase a long dead piece of lighting history let me offer a few hints for the practical minded person on how to bring this object back to life again.

The oil lamp illustrated in the photo to the right is a late Victorian duplex (twin wick burner) with opaque glass fount, Corinthian stand supported by a fluted brass section resting on a ceramic base. I'll direct these hints using this lamp as an example. Other lamps should be handled in a similar way, burners will differ but essentially the same steps should be taken.

Make sure to wear the appropriate protective clothing and accessories.

The first step is to disassemble the lamp, but please take heed, if you do not feel competent that you can retrace the procedure and put the item back together again at a later time please do not attempt to do this!

The parts of this lamp from the base up are:- ceramic base, fluted stand support, base column connector, Corinthian column, column top coupling, brass fount connector fitted to fount and fount with brass collar fitted to its top.

The basic rule is, never force anything. Okay, here we go.

Remove the burner.

Gently unscrew the fount from the stand and put in a place of safety. Sometimes you may need an assistant to hold the stand whilst you do this but don't try to force the thread as sometimes founts have been directly connected to the central connecting rod during their history. This has usually been done if the coupling's thread has become damaged or if a new coupling of an incorrect size has been used. If the fount will not unscrew use the following procedure.

Turn the lamp upside-down, rest it on its brass collar and gently loosen the Victorian nut under the base. Pushing gently down holding the Corinthian column remove the nut and any washers, then carefully remove the heavy ceramic base from the central connecting rod.

Next remove the fluted stand rest. Sometimes these can be fixed to the threaded connecting rod by another nut and washer which will need undoing.

Withdraw the Corinthian column, then to make it easier to wash the fount the central rod can be unscrewed from the top stand coupling which is connected to the fount supporter. Mole grips can be used for this operation if necessary, but if there is too much resistance it could mean the rod has been soldered in as an old repair so leave it intact. The fount will then have to be washed with the rod still connected.

If the fount has been removed with no problems – which is usually the case - undo the base nut with the stand assembly on its side and gently disconnect the parts.

Inspect all the brass parts for damage or cracking. Sometimes a little solder is needed to seal a crack here and there. Ordinary solder is fine for this as silver solder is quite hard to use and needs more heat. I'm not going into great detail about soldering as this is either something you will or will not be able to do so I'll be brief.

The way I would go about fixing a small crack in the base of a column or similar would be to first clean the immediate area inside and outside with wire wool then apply solder with a small iron to both surfaces. I'd then polish off the excess outside with a polishing disk using a 'Dremel' or similar tool and finally buff and then polish the repair with metal polish. Sometimes a repair like this can be almost invisible. The solder on the inner surface can usually be left untouched.

Okay let's clean up the lamp. Fount first.

Cleanup? Can you tell which is before and after?

There are many more lurid examples of distressed oil lamps than this, yes. But I tried to pick a slightly different example from the typical filthy black sticky and corroded ordinary brass table lamp which shines up like new after a good polish.

It is amazing how good a glass fount can look after a thorough clean. Invariably when you have acquired a lamp the fount will be filthy inside and out. Inside black 100 year old or more lamp oil residue can be stuck to the glass which will make it look dull and lifeless from the outside. It will probably also smell utterly revolting!

As mentioned in the previous chapter make sure you use cool water for cleaning and rinsing – room temperature is best.

Please take great care not to make any knocking movements when cleaning the inside of a glass fount. From past personal experience, to find you have managed to knock a large hole in the side of a rare fount I can assure you makes one feel more than a little unhappy! Not a good thing to do!

I usually use a plastic washing up brush – the type with a brush of about 6cm by 3cm and a chisel end rather than the fat bristly type. Wet the inside (room temperature water) then empty all the water out. Squirt in some cream cleaner and gently ease the brush through the burner collar. Clean thoroughly. If the sides need cleaning and the bristles won't reach I push in a wodge of damp kitchen paper, soak it with the cream cleaner already inside, and work it round with the chisel end of the brush. If there is nasty congealed paraffin glob that won't shift inside I use a 'Spontex' pan scourer the same way, not a brillo pad or wire wool but the type that's full of little round holes. They're good at cleaning and are gentle on the glass.

Of course there is an easier way to clean out grime, but it is a way I personally chose not to use. Commercial de-greasers are widely available on the web but if you decide to go this way make sure you use them in a well ventilated area and wear the appropriate protective clothing, goggles and mask. Although it's a brilliant de-greaser try to avoid anything Trichloroethylene based as it can also cause skin disease and health problems if inhaled!

For cleaning the outside of a fount it is best not to use a brush if there is any hand painting or gilding applied. Just use a water soaked soft cloth with a squirt of dishwashing liquid directly on to it. Rinse well both inside and out and dry with paper towels, finishing off by buffing up with a soft dry cloth.

The top collar and base brass connector will require a hand polish with 'Brasso' wadding or similar.

Clean your brass or other metal founts the same way making sure there are no pinholes through the metal where lamp oil can leak from. If there are pin holes and you wish to use the lamp it is best to have a professional metal worker repair them. Bear in mind that lamp oil is inflammable and a leaking lamp is dangerous. Commercial tank sealers are available but a tank – or fount – must be clinically clean inside before a repair can have a chance of being permanent. Personally, if I had a lamp with a holed fount I would not be prepared to take the risk of lighting it and keep it purely for decoration.

Brass founts will also require some 'elbow grease' by hand polishing.

Next step is to bring your burner back into good working order.

Photo above - Duplex burner parts (uncleaned)

To be efficient a burner's air intakes and filters need to be clean, the wick winders must run smoothly and the parts must be free from gunk and muck.

To achieve as perfect a state as possible we will take the burner apart. Again if you are not sure you have the skills to do this and then reassemble it please do not try. Clean the filters and inner parts to the best of your ability whilst removing no more than the top burner cover.

I am again using a duplex burner as example. Other types are similar in principle but parts will differ.

First step.

- Remove the burner top cover – the piece with the wick separator slots – and put to one side.

- Using long bladed pliers withdraw the securing pin from the snuffer mechanism's lever. Withdraw the lever and slide the mechanism off the burner sheaths. Make sure to note whether the lever has to be withdrawn from the inner or outer part of the burner, you will need to replace it the same way. The outside of the snuffer lever is always replaced with the curve pointing downwards.

- Gently remove the mesh bug filter from the inner base of the burner.

Next check all the parts for damage. A large amount of snuffer mechanisms have small slivers of supple metal which flex against the top flaps causing them to close over the wicks when raised. Sometimes one, or both can be missing. The easiest way to replace these is to purchase an old beyond repair burner from an auction site and raid it for spare parts. Occasionally I have even manufactured one by cutting a sliver from an old tin can and shaping it with scissors. It makes for an adequate – but not absolutely perfect - repair.

If the burner is the kind with vertical ventilation slots in the side and a few of these have cracks at the top or bottom, when the burner is clean these can be touched up from the inside with a small soldering iron and ordinary solder and smoothed over with the 'Dremel' and polishing disk.

Invariably a burner will be absolutely filthy. There are many ways to clean up the horrible mess. I'll just go into the two I use mainly.

The first is a method I sometimes use for exceptional and rare burners. I don't need to go into much detail about this as it just involves soaking the parts for sometimes quite a long time in a liquid called 'Horolene concentrated clock cleaner' used by watch and clock restorers. It is not cheap to purchase but works well. This can be found on the web and can be used in various dilutions – the stronger it is the quicker it will work. When the job is done the parts will be shining and spotless and will need no further polishing.

The following method is one I use quite a lot and works well although usually there is some buffing with metal polish needed to finish the job.

It is cheap and easy but sometimes time consuming.

Purchase some ordinary (Tesco's own brand is sensibly priced and good) colourless distilled vinegar and pour about three quarter full into an old cooking pot no longer in service for culinary use. The size of pot will be determined by the diameter of the parts you are going to clean.

Heat this until it is just off the boil and carefully place the part to be cleaned into the hot liquid. I use a long bladed pair of pliers for this purpose. Leave for about 8 to 10 minutes and remove with the pliers. As well as cleaning muck and tarnish from the part it will also take off any old varnish. If there was varnish on the part it may require another application later after the rinse and clean.

Rinse in clean hot water. At this stage we will finish the operation with a washing up brush and or old toothbrush with a liberal amount of cream cleaner applied. You will be amazed at the amount of filth which will come off and usually the rinsing water will be black within minutes. Clean everything including carefully scrubbing the bug filter with a toothbrush. Don't forget the inside of the burner top, the inside of the chimney clasps can also be carefully worked on with a slim toothbrush. Also clean the part below where the bug filter will be replaced and between the wick sheaths. The snuffer mechanism is perfect for the toothbrush also. For the inside of the flat wick sheaths I have a tiny bottle brush and clean well with cream cleaner.

Then rinse all parts thoroughly in running water, especially the inside of the wick sheaths making sure you spin the winder knobs to clear any vinegar from the inside. If this is not done properly the vinegar will impose itself on your senses at a later date!

Dry and rebuild the burner. Sometimes a burner will benefit from an application of metal polish and a buff. Sometimes this will not be necessary and the restored item will glow with pride as soon as it is assembled.

Sometimes you may wish to clean the various stand parts by this method. It can be a lot quicker than a laborious session with brass cleaner.

One word of warning. Do not overuse the vinegar. If it has got to the stage when it has become black and dirty it can leave a coppery deposit on your brass. This can reasonably easily be polished off with metal polish... but why add work?

Needless to say protective gloves are necessary with these procedures to stop your hands becoming impregnated and ingrained with filthy black stuff!

Basically that is all there is to it – at least about all that can be achieved in an ordinary household. There is nothing really complicated about an oil lamp, they come from the age of simplicity and non standardisation.

So there we are then, we seem to have reached the end.

I hope you've enjoyed working through this guide and have gleaned some useful information.

All the very best with your lamp collection and restoration, and remember to occasionally glance at my website... just in case... http://www.theoillampstore.com

Beautiful Oil Lamps

1920s Single wick table lamp

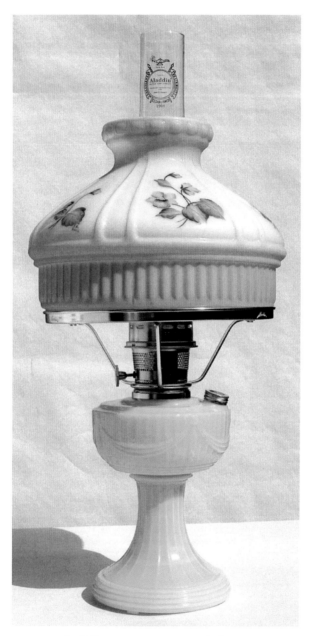

Aladdin Moonstone table lamp

Brass duplex table lamp with bonnet shade

Rowatt's Anucapnic lamp and chimney shade

Victorian Hinks ceramic drop in fount lamp

Brass and Copper stand duplex table lamp

Flower painted fount duplex table lamp

Coronaware ceramic single wick table lamp

Cut glass bracket peg wall lamp

Young's duplex cut glass fount table lamp

Victorian cranberry duplex table lamp and stand

Beautiful cranberry pink duplex table lamp

Ceramic drop in fount table lamp with closed tulip shade

Candy glass fount table lamp

Lovely green ceramic table lamp cut glass shade

Thank you so much for reading my book. I hope you really liked it and found the information useful.

As you probably know, many people look at the reviews on Amazon before they decide to purchase a book.

If you enjoyed the read could you take a minute to leave a review at Amazon with your feedback?

60 seconds is all I'm asking for, and it would mean the world to me.

Thank you so much

Myles Bevis

2 short stories by Myles Bevis
available on Amazon

A Lamp Called Jeannie – a twist of humour
The Crystal Set – A Mystery

Author's website http://www.theoillampstore.com

Author's blog http://ericbeemer.com

Made in the USA
Middletown, DE
07 November 2020